The Angler's
Quotation Book

I have gathered a posie of other men's flowers, and
nothing but the thread that binds them is mine own.

MONTAIGNE

The Angler's
Quotation Book

Edited by

ERIC RESTALL

ROBERT HALE • LONDON

Robert Hale Limited
Clerkenwell House
Clerkenwell Green
London EC1R 0HT

In loving memory
of a very dear friend, Eleanor

Printed and bound by Bookbuilders Limited
Hong Kong

Preface

The notion of angling as a highly developed art or sport, despite references to the taking of fish in the Old Testament and pictorial evidence from early Egypt, is of comparatively recent origin in Europe. Izaac Walton's Compleat Angler (1653) was by no means the first English work on the subject but its importance, and indeed dominance, is without parallel in the realms of sporting literature. The book which was enlarged and revised by the author, with contributions from his friends, during the remainder of his long life, is a curious mixture of practical advice interspersed with folklore, pastoral descriptions of the idyllic life, ballads, quotations, poems, anecdotes and even recipes. By the fifth edition (1676) the work had nearly doubled in size. This particular version is notable for the addition of a second part by Charles Cotton who extended Walton's instruction in fly-fishing and the making of flies.

Walton (1593-1683), quoting his dear friend Sir Harry Wotton, gave us a timeless explanation for the fascination of the sport: 'an employment for his idle time, which was then not idly spent . . . a rest to his mind, a cheerer of his spirits, a diverter of sadness, a calmer of unquiet thoughts, a moderator of passions, a procurer of contentedness; and that it begat habits of peace and patience in those that professed and practised it'. Such a multitude of virtues doubtless explains why angling has a following of nearly four million, making it the most popular by far of all participant sports.

In retrospect my initiation into the 'the gentle craft' at a very tender age is best described by that ungenerous quotation attributed to Samuel Johnson, 'a stick and a string, with a worm at one end and a fool at the other'.

My first experience of deep-sea fishing consisted of thirty minute's angling followed by three blissful hours of deep sleep, induced by the gentle rocking motion of the boat at anchor in combination with the wafting of diesel fumes.

Fly-fishing 'a very pleasant amusement', to quote the Doctor again, came much later to me, but that is another and a continuing story.

ERIC RESTALL

Acknowledgements

Grateful acknowledgement is made to the Fishmongers' Company, and their Archivist/Librarian Miss Meryl Beamont, for access to the Robert Bright Marston collection in the Company's library; to Miss Pamela Street who very generously provided two quotations of her late father the broadcaster and writer, A.G. Street; and a host of friends who searched their libraries, and their minds, for sources and quotes, including Martin Kendall, Brian Rakes, Steve Taplin, Joanna Restall-Young, Geoffrey Williams, Kina Restall, Bryone Picton, Shirley Day and many others.

Thanks are also due to the following for permission to include copyright material: Hugh Stoker, Sea Angling Hotspots; J.H. Russell and The Orvis Company Inc.; Mick Lunn, A Particular Lunn; Stanley Paul Ltd and Random House UK Ltd for extracts from Fly-fishing by J.R. Hartley; David Court and Blakes Holidays Ltd for an extract and a cartoon from Let's Be Broad Minded by Dennis Rooke; A. & C. Black Ltd for extracts from Advanced Coarse Fishing by Graham Marsden and Minor Tactics of the Chalk Stream by G.E.M. Skues; Springwater Publications for *extracts from* Stillwater Trout Fly-fishers' Ready Reference *by Peter Lightfoot and Kevin Whay; Little, Brown & Co. (UK) Ltd for an extract from* Salmon *by Arther Oglesby; Edmund J. Mason, Wye Valley; Victor Gollancz, an imprint of Cassell PLC, for an extract from* Daggie Dogfoot *by Dick King-Smith; Lyons & Burford Publishers for an extract from* The Masters on the Nymph *by J. Michael Migel and Leonard M. Wright, jun.; the extract from* The Observer's Book of Fly Fishing *by Peter Wheat is reproduced by permission of Frederick Warne & Co.; the extract from Henry Williamson's* Salar the Salmon *appears by permission of the Henry Williamson Literary Estate and the publisher, Faber & Faber Ltd; The Crowood Press for an extract from* Reflections From the Water's Edge *by John Bailey; the extract from* Coarse Fishing for Absolute Beginners *by Tag Barnes appears by courtesy of MacMillan Publishing, a division of MacMillan, Inc; extract of an article in the Daily* Telegraph, *7 August 1992, by Jonathan Young, appears by the writer's permission; The Crowood Press for extracts from* Dark Pools *by Charles Jardine and* Trout on a Nymph *by John Roberts; Blandford, a division of Cassell PLC, for an extract from* Specimen Hunter's Year Book *by Chris Yates; Quintet Publishing Ltd for an extract from* Fly Fishing *by Stephen Widsor; Times Newspapers Ltd for extracts from articles by John Young, The Times 13 August 1992, Derek Harris, The Times 3 August 1992 and Brian Clarke, The Times 15 October 1992; Lennard Associates for an extract from Eric Morecambe's* On Fishing; *the extract from Beatrix Potter's* The Tale of Mr Jeremy Fisher *appears by permission of Frederick Warne & Co.; Unwin Hyman, an imprint of HarperCollins Publications Ltd, for extracts from Frank Sawyer's* Keeper of the Stream; *Link House Magazines and*

Peter Warwick for an extract by David Jacques from The Angler's Annual 1973; *HarperCollins Publishers Ltd for extracts from* Border Reflections *by Lord Home of Hirsel; extracts by Frank Murgett and Alistair Ross from* The Third Angling Times Book (1963) *are reproduced by kind permission of Keith Higginbottom, editor of* Angling Times; *the wanted poster on page 57 and an extract from an article by John Fitzpatrick are included by permission of the* Evening Standard; *the extract from Norman Maclean's* A River Runs Through It *appears by permission of Pan Macmillan Publishers Ltd; the extract from Larry Koller's* The Treasury of Angling, © 1963 by Western Publishing Co. Inc., *is used by permission of the publisher; the extract from Ernest Hemingway's* To Have and Have Not *appears by permission of the Hemingway Foreign Rights Trust.*

The art of angling, or catching fish by a rod and line, is of very ancient derivation. The earliest writer upon it in our country was the Dame Juliana Berners, who wrote a treatise ['Treatyse of Fysshynge wyth an Angle'] on it in the *Boke of St. Albans*, printed by Wynkyn de Worde in 1496. Between that time and the present there have been nearly a thousand books, or part of books, written and published upon this subject.

Encyclopaedia Britannica, 1875

When a man is fishing, he can forget he has a religion, a political faith; he can forget noise, he can even forget income tax. Nothing matters except the little patch of water within reach of his fly. Look! There's a rise under that willow tree. What more do you want?

A.G. STREET
Any Questions?

Part of fishing's appeal to me is in its being a lonely and self-contained sport. You are absorbed in the music of waters, the beauty of the environment, the river's changing character, and the search for taking fish.

GARETH EDWARDS
On Fishing

Fishing serves the dual purpose both of concentrating the mind and liberating it.

LUDOVIC KENNEDY

Angling makes old men young and young men happy.

'FADDIST'
Freshwater Angling

11

Angling is not just a pastime or pursuit; it is an obsession
bordering on fanaticism. Indeed your true angler can only
be described as an addict.

TIMOTHY BENN
The (Almost) Compleat Angler

It [angling] deserves commendations; . . . it is an art, and
an art worthy the knowledge and practice of a wise man.

IZAAK WALTON
The Compleat Angler

The art of angling is an epitome of the game of life itself:
we are all anglers on a large scale.

T.E. PRITT
An Angler's Basket, 1896

Fishing has always been a progressive pursuit; it has always had a special attraction for the leisure of the intellectual.

> JOHN WALLER HILLS
> *A Summer on the Test*

Oh, the fisher's gentle life
Happiest is of any;
'Tis full of calmness, void of strife,
And beloved of many:
Other joys
Are but toys,
Only this
Harmless is,
For our skill
Breeds no ill,
But content and pleasure.

> JOHN CHALKHILL
> 'The Fisher's Life'

No other sport requires a greater awareness of the countryside in general and the watery environment in particular. No angler merely watches nature in a passive way. He enters into its very existence.

> JOHN BAILEY
> *Reflections from the Water's Edge*

Sir Henry Wotton . . . was also a most dear lover, and a frequent practiser of the art of angling; of which he would say, 'it was an employment for his idle time, which was then not idly spent . . . a rest to his mind, a cheerer of his spirits, a diverter of sadness, a calmer of unquiet thoughts, a moderator of passions, a procurer of contentedness; and that it begat habits of peace and patience in those that professed and practised it.'

> IZAAK WALTON
> *The Compleat Angler*

Angling: incessant expectation, and perpetual disappointment.

> ARTHUR YOUNG
> *Travels in France*

Man's life is but vain, for 'tis subject to pain
    And sorrow and short as a bubble;
'Tis a hodge-podge of business and money and care
    And care and money and trouble.

But we'll take no care when the weather proves fair,
    Nor will we now vex though it rain;
We'll banish all sorrow, and sing till tomorrow,
    And angle and angle again.
> ANON. c.1620

Fishing, if I, a fisher may protest,
Of pleasures is the sweetest of sports the best,
Of exercises the most excellent,
Of recreations the most innocent;
But now the sport is marde, and wott ye why?
Fishes decrease, and fishers multiply.
      THOMAS BASTARD, 1598

The fishing fever is easy to contract (one gets a few fish
and is oneself caught) and almost impossible to cure.
      'FADDIST'
      Freshwater Angling

Fishing is different from all other things. It is concerned
with so much more than just the physical facts; the centre
of it is really a state of mind.
      BERNARD VENABLES
      Freshwater Fishing

We may say of angling, as Dr Boteley said of strawberries,
'Doubtless God could have made a better berry, but
doubtless never did': and so if I might be the judge, God
never did make a more calm, quiet innocent recreation
than angling.
      IZAAK WALTON
      The Compleat Angler

15

It is a grand sport, a noble sport; it is the only sport of which can be said that the man who can wander about a riverside in thunder, lightning, hail, rain, wind, and snow, or sit all day without bite or sup on a wet sod in a cramp-inviting position, surrounded by fog thick with influenza, asthma, and rheumatic gout, is the same man who cannot be induced to go to church because the pews are uncomfortable.

T.E. PRITT
An Angler's Basket, 1896

Past times and present, equally prove that learned and good men - those pre-eminently distinguised for amenity of temper and piety of life - have been lovers of the art of angling.

T.C. HOFLAND
The British Angler's Manual, 1841

It has been gravely said that a good angler must also be a good Christian.

> H. CHOLMONDELEY-PENNELL
> *The Modern Practical Angler*

Of all the world's enjoyments
  That ever valued were,
There's none of our employments
  With fishing can compare.

> THOMAS D'URFEY

Patience and hope are two cardinal virtues in anglers especially, and, like original sin and the whooping-cough, every angler has 'em some time or other.

> T.E. PRITT
> *An Angler's Basket*, 1896

The pleasures of fishing are chiefly to be found in rivers, lakes and tackle shops and, of the three, the last are the least affected by the weather.

> ARTHUR RANSOME

There is more to fishing than catching fish.

> HUGH FALKUS
> *Sea Trout Fishing*

Many years back than I care to remember, my mother said of an uncle: 'He's a lazy man. He goes fishing.'

The public image of we anglers is distorted. They look upon us as either fools or layabouts, but we, of course, know differently.

FRANK MURGETT
The Third Angling Times Book

The value of night fishing is as a sedative to fretted nerves and a tired brain. A sedative, yet something more, a portal of escape from the instancy of the present.

T.C. KINGSMILL MOORE
A Man May Fish

Perhaps the greatest attraction of angling is that it demands so much thought, and perseverance, and skill, without imposing penalties for failure.

RICHARD WALKER & MAURICE INGHAM
Drop Me A Line

Like the pleasing volume of the patriarch of anglers - Izaak Walton - volumes might be written to point out and to depicture the beautiful scenery of woods and water sides, in the midst of which the pleasures attendant upon this exhilarating and health-restoring, hungry, exercise is pursued. How many narratives of the exploits of the day thus spent might be raked up to dwell upon, when they are all over, like a pleasing dream!

THOMAS BEWICK (1753-1828)
Memoir, 1862

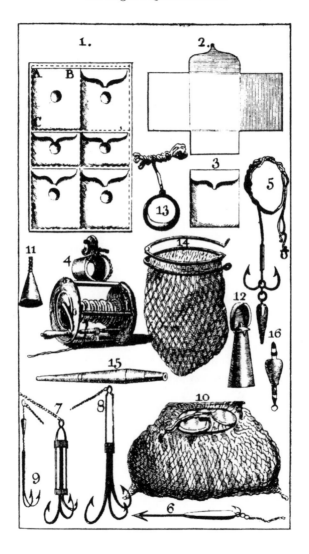

The image inherited from Father Izaak (may he rest in peace) depicts a world of angling as a bucolic paradise of perpetual sunshine, of singing milkmaids, of lavender scented bed-linen and of pure crystal streams. Majestically he ignored the overcast sky, the driving rain, the howling wind and the concealed bankside pothole.

> DAVID JACQUES
> *Angler's Annual*, 1973

Fishing is like Jason's quest for the Golden Fleece.

> ZANE GREY

You might find angling to be like the virtue of humility, which has a calmness of spirit and a world of blessings attending upon it.

> IZAAK WALTON
> *The Compleat Angler*

For there is no doubt that fishing cultivates patience, rather in the same way as walking stimulates thought.

> H.E. BATES

Fishing consists of a series of misadventures interspersed by occasional moments of glory.

> HOWARD MARSHALL
> *Reflections on a River*

And still the fair conceit I'd hold
That fishermen never grow old,
That with the daffodil's gold,
That, with the cowslip's plenty
And with the loud and building rooks
The men of rods and lines and hooks
Is always one-and-twenty.

PATRICK R. CHALMERS

It was always a mistake to believe that fishing, especially
trout fishing, called for patience. It is, of course, a fever,
an all-consuming lust that can brook neither opposition
nor interruption.

LOGIE BRUCE LOCKHART
The Pleasures of Fishing

He that will be an expert angler, must be endued with the
following qualifications: PATIENCE, DILIGENCE and
RESOLUTION.

Patient, to endure the disappointments that attend
anglers, who cannot promise to themselves, at all times,
the desired success; diligent, in following such
instructions as shall be communicated to him, observing
the various seasons of the year, and various dispositions of
fish; resolute, to rise early, and pursue his sport, whether it
be hot or cold, in winter or in summer.

The Angler's Guide, 1828

Patience must be moderated to promote the art, and time procrastinated to proclaim the angler an artist.
RICHARD FRANCK, 1694

As no man is born an artist,
So no man is born an angler.
IZAAK WALTON
The Compleat Angler

In fishing, anticipation is the pleasure; the capture the thrill.
ERNEST A. ARIS
Fishing

There are two kinds of fisherman; those who fish for sport and those who catch something.
ANON.

Anticipation is one of the delights of fishing.
MAURICE HEADLAM
A Holiday Fisherman

Bosses do not love anglers. They find that on mild days, especially early in the season, there is a suspiciously high incidence of bad backs and dead grandmas.
CLIFF PARKER
Hook, Line and Stinker

Fishing is in many ways like chess. Although there are set rules governing how the pieces move, there is no end to the subtleties of play or limits to the gambits involved. One is always learning.

> JOHN ASHLY-COOPER
> *A Salmon Fisher's Odyssey*

Anticipation is a prime ingredient of the pleasures of fishing. From those first days when I propped my bicycle against the mill race fence and untied my rod case from the crossbar, I have approached the water as if it were some alluring parcel waiting to be unwrapped. As you grow older you contain to some degree the eagerness to get going, you take longer in the preparation, not just because you're conscious of fish lost through casts too quickly tied but because too there is a pleasure merely in extending anticipation.

> J.R. HARTLEY
> *Fly Fishing*

It is our lost fish that I believe stay longest in our memory, and seize upon our thoughts whenever we look back to fishing days. The most gallant fish when eaten is forgotten, but the fish that, after a mad, glorious battle, has beaten us and left us quivering with excitement and vexation, is hooked and lost again in many a year to come.

> A.H. CHAYTOR
> *Letters to a Salmon Fisher's Sons*

It [fly casting] is an art that is performed on a four-count rhythm between ten and two o'clock.

> NORMAN MACLEAN
> *A River Runs Through It*

Fly-fishing is an intensely personal sport and each one of us seeks from it different pleasures and goals.

> JEREMY LUCAS
> *Fly-Fisher*

DRY FLY FISHING; the great safety valve of strenuous life

> Advertisement in
> *The Fishing Gazette*, Saturday 13 August, 1910

This peculiar and almost immediate relief which this innocent pursuit [fly-fishing] yields to the distressed or uneasy mind, by calming the perturbations which misfortunes or other vexatious circumstances may have excited, is to be ranked amongst the first of its recommendations.

> GEORGE C. BAINBRIDGE
> *The Fly Fisher's Guide,* 1816

The book plate of Robert Bright Marston, sometime editor of *Fishing Gazette*, honorary treasurer of the Flyfisher's Club and editor of the one hundredth edition of *The Compleat Angler*.

Founded in 1822, the Houghton Club was and always will be a fellowship of anglers dedicated to the pursuit of the trout with the fly.

> MIKE LUNN with CLIVE GRAHAM-RANGER
> *A Particular Lunn*

The Test gives all sorts of water - the slow glide, the quick stream, the easy cast behind a convenient tussock, the difficult ones round a willow, across a weedbed, into a patch where the current runs different ways - the variety is infinite.

> MAURICE HEADLAM
> *Rod, Horn and Gun*

The earliest reference to fishing with the artificial fly
They fasten red wool round a hook and fix on to the wool
two feathers which grow under a cock's wattles, and
which in colour are like wax. Their rod is six feet long
and their line of the same length. Then they throw their
snare and the fish, maddened and excited by the colour,
come straight at it, thinking by the sight to get a dainty
mouthful; when, however, it opens its jaws, it is caught by
the hook and enjoys a bitter repast, a captive.

    CLADIUS AELIAN
    De Natura Animalium, c. 200AD

I have seene a younge flie swimme in the water too and
fro, and in the end, come to the upper-curst of the river,
and assay to flie up: howbeit, not being perfectly ripe or
fledged, hath thrice fallen down againe into the bottome:
howbeit, in the end receiving perfection by the heate of
the sunne, and the pleasant fat water, hath in the ende
within some halfe houre after taken her flyte, and flied
quite away into the ayre, and of such young flies before
they are able to flie away, do fish feede exceedingly.

    JOHN TAVERNER
    Certaine Experiments Concerning Fish and Fruite,
    1600

In 1910, when dry-fly purism was at its height, G.E.M. Skues published a book called *Minor Tactics of the Chalk Stream* which let loose the most virulent controversies that even the sport of angling, a natural breeding ground for such battles, never produced before or since.

The fly was fished under the water, and that, in the eyes of the purists (Halford and his followers) was the sin against the Holy Ghost. Skues was the subject of an attack that consisted of everything from sharp criticism to wild abuse. Yet in the end he triumphed, as he had to.

LARRY KOLLER
The Treasury of Angling

There are those who wax indignant at the use of the wet-fly on dry-fly water. Yet it has a special fascination. The indications which tell your dry-fly angler when to strike are clear and unmistakable, but those which bid a wet-fly man to raise his rodpoint and draw in the steel are frequently so subtle, so evanescent and impalpable to the senses, that, when the bending rod assures him that he has divined aright, he feels an ecstacy as though he had performed a miracle each time.

G.E.M. SKUES

Minor Tactics of the Chalk Stream

The feud reached its climax in a famous encounter at the Flyfisher's Club, when an ageing Halford and his curia of disciples cornered the younger Skues in the foyer.

'Young man,' Halford said testily, 'you cannot fish the Itchen in the manner you describe.'

'But I've done it,' Skues replied softly.

J. MICHAEL MIGEL & LEONARD M. WRIGHT, JUN.
The Masters on the Nymph

Fishing the sunk fly is an exacting and entrancing an art as fishing the dry; in fact I am not sure that fishing it upstream when you cannot see your fish is not the highest art of all.

JOHN WALLER HILLS
A Summer on the Test

Many anglers regard nymph fishing as a fad which will run its course and, in due time, be forgotten. This may to some extent prove true. It is more difficult than dry-fly fishing and many anglers, having had no success with nymphs, have gone back to their dry flies, discarding the nymph as just one more gadget. But there are times when the nymphs, although difficult to handle, are invaluable in the taking of trout which otherwise would not be caught.

EDWARD RINGWOOD HEWITT
& JOHN ALDEN KNIGHT
The Modern Angler, 1936

This process of refining the way they fish is something that affects most fishermen as they develop and grow older. As for me, now that I am as old as a can of beans, my remaining ambitions are compressed into one supreme sequence. It begins with me tying my own flies - unlikely now, because the hands are getting stiff, but no matter, this is Dreamland. Then I go down to the river. It is a perfect summer day. I stalk the bank and find this mesmerizingly beautiful Brown Trout. I cast for it, the fly lands spot on, and this magnificent fish slowly, inexorably (whatever that means) rises through the gin-clear water and takes it. I play my superb prize, reel it in, take a long wondering look at it, and fall dead in the water.

What better way could there be of making sure that you arrive at the Gates of Heaven with a smile on your face?

ERIC MORECAMBE
On Fishing

I have often been accused in my method of greased line fishing for salmon of letting the fly drift downstream motionless, having got rid of all drag; but when you can see the fly you will see that every little eddy it floats down through gives the fly little twists and movement, just the same as some live insect would do, and that is one of the reasons why I wish to avoid what you call drag, and although the fly may be passing across the stream and downstream at the same time it behaves in a very natural way and there is no tension on the line.

A.H.E. WOOD , 1939

Is there anything to beat a day's fishing in our Wiltshire water meadows in July? If there is, I have never known it.

A.G. STREET
Hedgetrimmings

I firmly believe that if God had wanted to create a water expressly for fly-fishers, it would certainly look similar to a chalk stream in May, a place of unparalleled loveliness.

CHARLES JARDINE
Dark Pools

One feels that the water-meadows are a little too soft, and that the air lacks freshness. The even-flowing chalk stream, the river which is so clear and gentle, so docile and perfectly under control, seems just a little tame, till at last there rises up before one's mind the full-formed images of rough noisy streams, and great brown pools clearing after a flood.

LORD GREY OF FALLODON

As I look at my perfectly shaped Test trout, his small head, his bright, broad silver body; as I feast my eyes on the clear water, the green reeds, and the glimpse of yellowing Downs beyond, I am all thankfulness to be where I am. One Test trout, fought and conquered, whether schemed for or fluked, is enough to make one forget Scotland.

MAURICE HEADLAM
A Holiday Fisherman

How little does he know of angling who has merely fished the preserved streams of fat and prosperous England.

DR KNOX
Fish and Fishing in the Lone Glens of Scotland, 1854

There is fishing in Shetland - wading in voes or casting with nervous precision into narrow burns - that paints a lustre on all one's memories of that grim and splendid archipelago; and the habit of fishing entices one into places of strange and desolate beauty.

ERIC LINKLATER
Orkney and Shetland

Can there be a trout fisherman who has watched a dun or olive floating down a stream without a feeling of anticipation, followed by a moment of excitement as a trout rises to suck the fly under the water?

ALASTAIR ROSS
The Third Angling Times Book

The old adage 'match the hatch' still rings as true today as ever it did. If a little, fluffy, green thing with white wings is fluttering about, try and fish something similar, or the nymph or pupa you think would be appropriate to it.

PETER LIGHTFOOT & KEVIN WHAY
Stillwater Trout Fly-Fishers' Ready Reference

All fish are not caught with flies.
>JOHN LYLY
>*Euphues*

You must lose a fly to catch a trout.
>GEORGE HERBERT
>*Jacula Prudentum*

The fish dies because he opens his mouth.

The closed mouth swallows no flies.
>SPANISH PROVERBS

An Angling Secret
On rough and wet days a large fly worked in jerks along
the top of the water is often very deadly.
>PAT CASTLE
>*Trout and How to Catch Them*

Here comes the trout that must be caught with tickling.
>SHAKESPEARE
>*Twelfth Night*

Here and there a lusty trout
And here and there a grayling.
>ALFRED LORD TENNYSON

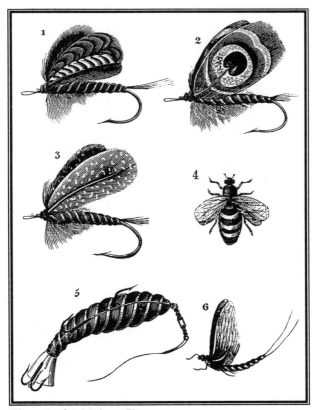

Three Artificial Salmon Flies.

1. Jay Fly for Salmon.

2. Peacock Fly for Salmon.

3. Silver Pheasant for Salmon.

4. Bee, a natural Bait for a Chub.

5. Devil, an Artificial Bait for Trout.

6. A natural May Fly, or Green Drake, a killing bait in dapping for Trout.

For trouts are tickled best in muddy water.
SAMUEL BUTLER

The best anglers seem to possess an ability to transcend the hard tangible reality of terra firma and submerge themselves mentally into this water dimension. They are the people one meets from time to time who fish an area shunned by all and, for no accountable reason, proceed to catch an abundance of large fish. They are the anglers who can tell by a sixth sense when a trout has taken a nymph, although nothing is seen, heard or felt. In short, they are guided by instinct and insight.
CHARLES JARDINE
Dark Pools

Trout are not to be caught with dry breeches.
SPANISH PROVERB

The prime cause of failure in dry-fly presentation is often not poor imitation of the fly but unseen or undetected drag. Of course on some occasions a reasonable imitation of the fly may be important, but to infer it is paramount is an old wives' tale.
ARTHUR OGLESBY
Reeling In

You can imitate the nymph, but you cannot imitate the wiggle.
GEORGE SELWYN MARRYAT
The Treasury of Angling

If the wet and heavy fly be exchanged for a dry and light one, and passed in artistic style over the feeding fish, it will, partly from the simple circumstances of its buoyancy, be taken, nine cases out of ten, as greedily as the living insect itself. We admit, however, to ensure this, imitation of the predominant species, at least as regards colour and size, is required.

GEORGE PULMAN
Vade-Mecum of Fly Fishing for Trout, 1841

I am in favour of an exact representation for dry-fly or nymph, but when I use the word representation I try to carry it into effect. I want representation that is satisfactory from the trout's point of view. A correct imitation of the colouring and shape of an insect is not enough. To represent truly an insect, and successfully deceive a trout, the artificial must be offered at a time when he is taking, or likely to be taking, the natural from or beneath the surface of the water; offered in such a manner that it looks alive, or dead, or in a semi-inert stage, as natural ones are at the moment.

FRANK SAWYER
Keeper of the Stream

It is said, perhaps with some truth, that presentation is far more important in stimulating a take than the pattern of the fly. Perhaps so but it seems to me that the two are to some extent indivisible, a partnership, in which one cannot be effective without the other.

CONRAD VOSS BARK
On Flyfishing

There are different opinions as to what constitutes the attractions to the fish of an artificial fly. Some say shape, some colour, some movement, some size, but these things must all be incorporated in a good imitation, or it is not a good imitation, for all these are part of the fly that is to be espied.

>ROGER WOOLLEY
>*Modern Trout Fly Dressing*

Among the many uncertainties which attend the sport of fly-fishing, there is one thing that may be laid down as certain, and that is that no consistent measure of success attends a lure, whether wet, dry or semi-submerged, in which the angler has not faith.

>G.E.M SKUES
>*Minor Tactics of the Chalk Stream*

My advice to anglers is always to have patience and offer the trout a selection of flies before giving up on it. If it's a really difficult fish and refuses every fly in your box, spit on the fly and see if the trout is prepared to take the fly just under the surface; nine times out of ten it will. Purists may not approve of this method, but it can make the difference between a blank day and a fish in the bag.

>MICK LUNN with CLIVE GRAHAM-RANGER
>*A Particular Lunn*

When you angle with an artificial fly, in slow-running rivers or still places, cast it across the water, and let it sink a little, and then draw it gently over to you again, letting the current carry it slowly down; this is the best way for slow rivers; but for quick ones, your fly must always swim on the top, under your continual inspection.

ROBERT HUISH
The Improved British Angler, 1838

There is only one theory about angling in which I have perfect confidence, and this is the two words, least appropriate to any statement about it, 'always' and 'never'.

LORD GREY OF FALLODON
Fly-fishing, 1899

The fly-fishing novice who goes out believing he is provided with an unrivalled collection of death-dealing tackle and flies which must certainly empty the river, is about as foolish as that other fellow who thinks a grass-widow is green.

T. E. PRITT
An Angler's Basket, 1896

The pleasure of a really good cast is almost orgasmic.
>   PETER HINTON-GREEN
>   *Ndeke Tales*

One of the first members to use a singlehanded rod and to stalk his fish used to relate how Mr Martin Tucker Smith, seeing him one day crawling on his knees, called out: 'Why are you crawling about like a snake in the grass? Why don't you stand up and fish like a man?'
>   *Chronicles of the Houghton Fishing Club*, 1908

Casting Accuracy

In most trout fishing, a careful approach and accurate casting is more important than distance casting. To practise accuracy, set a paper plate in your garden and practise dropping a dehooked fly on it from 20-25 feet away.
>   ORVIS CATALOGUE, 1992

The great error of fly-fishing, as it is usually practised . . . is that the angler fishes downstream whereas he should fish up.
>   WILLIAM C. STEWART
>   *The Practical Angler*, 1857

Quite three parts in four of fishing consist in keeping out of sight and making the least possible disturbance in the water; therefore fish up-stream all the time and every time.

> PAT CASTLE
> *Trout and How to Catch Them*

To be a fly fisherman is both a joy and an affliction. Few more testing yet delightful ways of catching a fish exist, and no one would choose to hunt their food in such a way if survival was their main obsession.

> STEPHEN WIDSOR
> *Fly Fishing*

If you cast your Fly up against the Stream, the Trout that lies upon the Fin in such strong Currents, and discerns you not, being behind him, presently takes your bait.

> JOHN WORLIDGE
> *Systema Agriculturae,* 1669

Fly-fishing has been compared, though by a somewhat circuitous mode of reasoning, to sculpture. It proceeds upon a few principles, and the theory is easily acquired, although it may require long and severe labour to become a great master in the art.

> JAMES WILSON
> *The Rod and the Gun,* 1861

Fly fishing has always been, and we believe always will be, the favourite method of angling; and deservedly so.

> WILLIAM C. STEWART
> *The Practical Angler,* 1857

I've met some fly fishers who could happily converse with a passing Roman centurion, such is their fluency in Latin. Because he struggled to ingrain *Amo, Amas, Amat* into me my old classics master would despair if he could hear me try to wrap my tongue around *Aphelocheirus montandoni*. Most trout speak English.

> JOHN ROBERTS
> *Trout on a Nymph*

Almost everyone is now-a-days a *piscator.* The *Fanatico,* about Easter, goes off as busy as the cockney on his nunter, when bound to Epping. He generally takes a great many things, and kills a few fish. The old angler takes a few things, and kills a great many fish.

About ninety in a hundred fancy themselves anglers. About one in a hundred *is* an angler. About ten in a hundred throw the hatchet better than a fly.

> PETER HAWKER
> *Instructions to Young Sportsmen*

After these delays I came to the ripple at the head of the pool, got a fly onto it at the twelfth attempt and was rewarded by the sort of 'wink under water' that recalls the proverb *Ars longa trutta brevis,* which means, the longer you take to cover a fish the shorter he rises.

> H. T. SHERINGHAM
> *Trout Fishing*

He [Will Wimble] is extremely well versed in all the little handicrafts of an idle man; he makes a May-fly to a miracle; and furnishes the whole country with angle-rods.

> JOSEPH ADDISON
> 'Coverley Papers', *The Spectator,* 4 July, 1711

Fly-fishing is certainly the most gentlemanly and pleasant kind of angling, and it has many advantages over every other kind of angling.

> T. C. HOFLAND
> *The British Angler's Manual,* 1841

Fly-fishing may be a very pleasant amusement; but angling or float fishing I can only compare to a stick and a string, with a worm at one end and a fool at the other.

> *Attributed to* SAMUEL JOHNSON

The take of a trout is always a bonus, a gift from the river god to be received humbly and with thanks.

> CONRAD VOSS BARK
> *On Flyfishing*

Fly rods are like women; they won't play if they're maltreated!

> CHARLES RITZ
> *A Fly Fisher's Life*

I am not particularly interested in killing trout. What does interest me immensely is catching trout by a method we call dry fly.

> DAVID JACQUES
> *Fisherman's Fly*

Fishing with an artificial fly is certainly a very pleasant and gentlemanly way of angling, and is attended with much less labour and trouble than bottom fishing.

> T. F. SALTER
> *The Angler's Guide*, 1815

Two anglers were fishing from a boat on an Irish lough, the surface of which was very placid, when a fine trout rose about twenty yards away, and one of the anglers, making a long cast, succeeded in dropping his tail fly into the middle of the widening rings on the water. In an instant the fish rose again at the angler's fly, and was struck and just touched, and then was gone.

'Tare an' ounds,' said the boatman. 'Ah! that was a grand fish yer honner. Yez'll not see the likes of that fish again to-day. Oh! be the powers, he was a fine gentleman, he was.'

'A big fish, was he Pat?'

'Troth, an' he was, sorr; he was the full of a door.'

'As large as that? Did you see him?'

'Shure, an' I did, sorr; troth, sorr, he was a rale treasure of a trout.'

'How big would he be, do you think?'

'Troth, sorr, I can't say to two foot; but your honner's clothes wouldn't have fitted him.'

T. E PRITT
An Angler's Basket, 1896

If you are fishing a floating line, the excitement of the fish coming up and taking it is tremendous. Then the line sinking and the thrill of it going up your arm when you come in contact.

LORD HOME

There is great truth in the saying that the best fly to use is the one you believe in.

> HUGH FALKUS
> *Sea Trout Fishing*

I recall standing on the bank of a lonely reservoir high up in the Breconshire hills one late summer's evening and admiring with intense satisfaction three beautifully marked trout lying on the wet stones of the shoreline. It had rained heavily all day. I was cold and soaked to the skin. And the fish averaged barely half a pound. Yet I remember feeling as happy then as at any moment in my life.

Is it any wonder that the mystical appeal of catching trout on artificial fly is so impossible to explain - that the only way of truly understanding it is to experience it for yourself?

> PETER WHEAT
> *The Observer's Book of Fly Fishing*

You might as well look for whiskers on sardines as expect to rise a good trout after he once had a fair look at you.

> T. E. PRITT
> *An Angler's Basket*, 1896

A trout that is not hungry will no more look at an angler's bait than a respectable man will look at a giblet pie.

> T. E. PRITT
> *An Angler's Basket*, 1896

Obviously, nothing works all the time - neither fly nor method. Flies that took fish today, may not do so tomorrow.

Yesterday is different from today, and tomorrow may be different still.

SIDNEY DU BROFF
Fly Fishing on Still Water

The old and young, the learned and ignorant, the poor and rich, all classes, ages and conditions have enjoyed angling for trout. Once, nearly every stream in the Middle, Northern and Eastern States teemed with both trout and salmon. The salmon has been driven away, and had not anglers interfered to save the trout, they would now be known only from books and from the stories of the older inhabitants.

LORENZO PROUTY
Fish: Their Habits and Haunts and the Methods of Catching Them, 1883

Whilst yielding to the Trout in courage and dash, the Grayling is yet a beautiful and mettlesome fish - a foeman not unworthy of our steel.

H. CHOLMONDELEY-PENNELL
The Modern Practical Angler

And for winter fly-fishing it is as useful as an almanac out
of date.

> IZAAK WALTON
> *The Compleat Angler*

As between the salmon and the trout I hesitate to express
a preference. The salmon has it for size and strength, but
the trout demands on the whole greater skill and finesse
from the fisherman.

> LORD HOME
> *Border Reflections*

Even though I have seen the same thing many times, the
sight once more of scores of trout spawning on the
shallows gives me the greatest of pleasure. Many of these
fish are of a sporting size, and amongst them are trout
which would grace any fisherman's basket during the
fishing season. It does me good to see the waves and
turmoil, the flashes as the light reflects from sides and
bellies, and dorsal and tail fins showing above the surface,
for I can picture these fish later on, waiting in some run or
eddy, under a branch or jutting bank, sucking in the
luckless flies which drift to them with the currents.

> FRANK SAWYER
> *Keeper of the Stream*

Fishing was hopeless, but I went out as usual, and, as I was walking along gossiping with the gillie, I suddenly saw a fine fresh-run sea-trout flapping about on some rocks in the middle of the stream. I told the gillie to put his net over it, and when he had tapped it on the head - it weighed just three pounds - I said to him: 'What fly did I catch that fish on?' He gazed at me solemnly for a second. 'It was a Claret,' he said. 'Tomorrow there will be dozens fishing with a Claret.'

No one else caught anything, of course, and I was considered a marvellous fisherman.

MAURICE HEADLAM
A Holiday Fisherman

The salmon is the noblest of fresh-water fish, and stands highest in the angler's estimation. He is king of the streams; his title to precedence has never yet been questioned; his magnitude, his keen and lively eye, his shining silvery scales, his muscular powers, his rapid and graceful motions, his beautiful proportions, his intellectual instincts, and his rich, delicate flavour, all unite in establishing his superiority over all other fish.

LORENZO PROUTY
Fish: Their Habits and Haunts and the Methods of Catching Them, 1883

Avoid standing upon rocking stones, for obvious reasons; and never go into water deeper than the fifth button of your waistcoat; even if this does not always agree with tender constitutions in frosty weather. As you are likely not to take a just estimate of the cold in the excitement of the sport, should you be of delicate temperament, and be wading in the month of February, when it may chance to freeze very hard, pull down your stockings, and examine your legs. Should they be black, or even purple, it might, perhaps, be as well to get on dry land; but if they are only rubicund, you may continue in enjoying the water, if it so pleases you.

WILLIAM SCROPE
Days and Nights of Salmon Fishing in the Tweed

Unfortunately it is still true to say that one of the greatest factors in successful salmon fishing is determined by the size of the angler's income balance. Those who can afford the best beats usually have a head start on lesser mortals.

ARTHUR OGLESBY
Salmon

Fly-fishers do more than politicians to promote friendliness between nations.

> Letter from an eminent American editor to
> Sir George Aston author of
> *Letters to Young Fly-Fishers*

The salmon fishing skills of HM the Queen Mother are well-chronicled and there can be few more determined anglers as indicated by the following incident. Having waited all day for conditions to improve, Her Majesty at last set out for the river in the early evening.

An anxious staff waiting to serve dinner, by which time it was already getting dark, assembled with torches to begin an urgent search of the river bank. The staff should have known better for just then Her Majesty appeared with a twenty-pounder in her grasp. With a bravado, only appreciated by the really dedicated angler, came the explanation for her absence. '*This* is what detained me!'

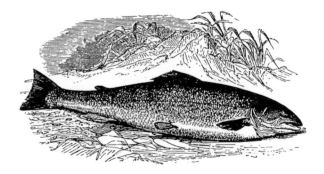

There is great pleasure to be found in fishing and even more in the realisation that fish can be put back unharmed once personal needs have been met.

>DEREK KNOWLES
>*Salmon on a Dry Fly*

In the gravel of the moorland stream the eggs were hatching, little fish breaking from confining skins to seek life, each one alone, save for the friend of all, the Spirit of the waters. And the star-stream of heaven flowed Westward, to far beyond the ocean where salmon, moving from deep water to the shallows of the islands, leapt - eager for immortality.

>HENRY WILLIAMSON
>*Salar the Salmon*

The salmon runs are a visible symbol of life, death and regeneration, plain for all to see and share . . . If there is ever a time when the salmon no longer returns, man will know he has failed again and moved one step nearer to his own final disappearance.

>RODERICK HAIG-BROWN

He began with a bare hook, a piece of fishing gut, and a few bits of silk and feathers; and lo, in about three minutes, there issued from his consummate manipulation a gorgeous fly, so beautiful, and, withal, so plump and appetising, that for a salmon to see it was to look and die.

>*A Little Tour in Ireland,* 1859

Robert Pashley, a renowned fisherman of the 1930s, in one year caught no fewer than forty tons of salmon, enough to fill a trawler. In those days the Wye was so full of salmon that it was almost possible to cross the river by stepping on them, surely an exaggeration, but now the number of salmon has been much depleted.

> EDMUND J. MASON
> *The Wye Valley*

The fisher constantly is as it were in a wild garden, and this very pleasure to be found in the beauty around him he has made a part of his sport itself. It has a spirit: it is not merely the sport of taking fish.

> A. H. CHAYTOR
> *Letters to a Salmon Fisher's Sons*

How can we be expected to take an interest in a country like Canada where the salmon do not rise to the fly?

> LORD MELBOURNE

'What a day! Two salmon this morning and the offer of the Exchequer this afternoon!'

> NEVILLE CHAMBERLAIN, a dedicated angler,
> declining Stanley Baldwin's invitation to
> become Chancellor of the Exchequer,
> 16 August 1933.

Anglers dream of pulling in a huge salmon from the turbulent waters of a Scottish sea loch. But many are turning their backs on the lochs because the fishing has become too easy - nearly every time, they seem to hook one of thousands of salmon freed from bankrupt fish farms. The fish, bred in protected waters, put up only the most feeble resistance.

ROSS CLARK
Daily Mail, 29 October 1992

Fordingbridge

Nowadays the little town is perhaps best known as headquarters for those brothers of the angle who come a-fishing in the troutful and pikeful waters of the Avon. The Avon cannot compete with Test and Itchen as a trout stream, but has the best salmon and coarse fishing the country has to offer.

D. H. MOUTRAY READ
Highways and Byways in Hampshire, 1908

The Germans have a tradition that when Christ was crucified all the fishes dived under the waters in terror, except the pike, which, out of curiosity, lifted up its head and beheld the whole scene; hence the fancy that in a pike's head all the parts of the Crucifixion are represented, the cross, three nails, and a sword being distinctly recognizable.

ANON.

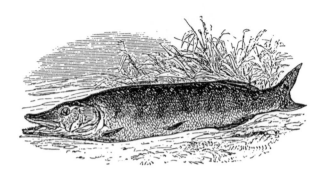

I know some who do angle for Bream and Pike with artificial flies, but I judge the labour lost and the knowledge a needless curiosity, those fish being taken much easier, especially the pike by other wayes.

ROBERT VENABLES
The Experienced Angler, 1662

In the late summer months and fine days in autumn, when the deeps are curled by a fine breeze, pike are to be taken very pleasantly by means of a fly. The best imitation is a very large one of a dragon fly. An imitation of the sand-martin or swallow, dressed by means of feathers on a large hook, will prove an attractive bait for pike in the seasons last mentioned.

EDWARD FITZGIBBON
A Handbook of Angling, 1847

The impression of streamlining, power and demoniac relentlessness given by his mouth, whether closed or open, is immense. A pike, indeed, arouses curious feelings of emnity for which I personally know of no parallel among English wild creatures.

H. E. BATES

You will hear tales of monsters; of leviathans; of ducks and even swans being dragged beneath the surface; of great, vicious heads that poke out of the water to shake the life out of a victim. You will hear every monster/maneater kind of tale there is to hear, sometime, somewhere, wherever you find pike.

GRAHAM MARSDEN
Advanced Coarse Fishing

There are few more pleasant ways of spending a fine autumn day than wandering along a slow-flowing river spinning for pike with plug, swallowtail or spoon.

CHARLES CHENEVIX TRENCH
A History of Angling

It was on Llandegfedd Reservoir in 1989 that Gareth Edwards, one of Wales' finest rugby players, made his name in angling. Edwards who is a fanatic fisherman, landed a pike weighing 45lb 6oz, so breaking the record for the species in England and Wales.

BRIAN CLARKE
The Times, 15 October 1992

As a party of Ladies and Gentlemen were angling in a pond at East Bergholt, in Suffolk, a dog belonging to one of them, went to the water, and whilst in the act of lapping, a large jack darted at the dog's tongue, and bit it through upon which the dog instantly gave a sudden jerk, and tossed the fish, which weighed 7lb and a quarter, out of the pond, to the great diversion of the company: the dog was so much hurt, that he howled most bitterly for a considerable time after.

The Times, 28 August 1790

Possibly there is something in the theory that pike feed on moonlit nights, all of them; and that a blank day means the quiescence of digestion after this communal feast. It is a sad theory for those of us who cannot await the moon's phases for our day's fishing.

MAURICE HEADLAM
Rod, Horn and Gun

Evening Standard, 12 August 1992

A £60 bounty is being offered to anyone who catches a giant pike, estimated to weigh more than 30lb which has eaten a goose and several ducks on the lake at Alexandra Park, north London.

JOHN YOUNG
The Times, 13 August 1992

The Freshwater Shark

The Pike is the tyrant of freshwater fish, and is accounted a longer liver than any other, except the Carp. The chief articles of his sustenance are frogs and fish, even those of his own species. The very large ones are so voracious, that they have been known to snap at the limbs of a boy when swimming, and at a dog or other animal; they will also draw down young geese, ducks, and other waterfowl under the water, and devour them.

> SAMUEL TAYLOR
> *Angling in All Its Branches,*
> *Reduced to a Complete Science*, 1800

I am not in favour of live baiting for pike; I think, if it is necessary that anything should suffer inconvenience, then let it be the pike - he has a brutal nature and it is only fitting that he should get a taste of his own medicine. No matter how well a live bait is arranged the little fish is bound to suffer, either in body through being attached to hooks, or in mind through being tethered and at the mercy of its greatest enemy.

> FRANK SAWYER
> *Keeper of the Stream*

I remember asking a Loch Leven boatman if the numerous pike in the loch often took the spinning baits of trout anglers. 'Dom them,' said he, 'the greedy brutes would tak' o' the Sawbath day.'

> T. E. PRITT
> *An Angler's Basket*, 1896

The angler must be careful not to put his hand where the pike can eat it. Pike love human hands, and many a careless angler has lost a hand, a leg, or a wallet containing his identity card and two ten-shilling notes in this way. Minnows and dace are less dangerous. Even a tench finds difficulty in swallowing a whole hand owing to the construction of its mouth, which is shaped like a mousehole.

> DENNIS ROOKE
> *Let's Be Broad-Minded!*

Jack, Pike, Salmon, Perch, Trout, Chub, Eels, etc destroy immense numbers of their brethren daily, and, by their tyranny, keep the whole inhabitants of the rivers, lakes, and ponds, in continual terror and alarm. The angler has frequent opportunities of observing the extreme distress and agitation of small fish when a Pike, or any other fish of prey, makes his appearance among them: on these occasions they are so much terrified and confused as sometimes to leap out of the water into a boat, or on the shore, to escape the fangs of their merciless pursuers, and avoid immediate destruction.

> T. F. SALTER
> *The Angler's Guide,* 1815

He has fished well and caught a frog.

> JOHN HEYWOOD
> *Proverbs*

Thus use your frog . . . Put your hook, I mean the arming-wire through his mouth, and out at his gills; and then with a fine needle and silk sew the upper part of his leg, with only one stitch, to the arming-wire of your hook; or tie the frog's leg, above the upper joint to the armed-wire; and, in so doing, use him as though you loved him.

IZAAK WALTON
The Compleat Angler

And angling, too, that solitary vice,
Whatever Izaak Walton sings or says;
The quaint, old, cruel coxcomb, in his gullet
Should have a hook, and a small trout to pull it.

It would have taught him humanity at least. This sentimental savage, whom it is a mode to quote (amongst novelists) to show their sympathy for innocent sports and old songs, teaches how to sew up frogs, and break their legs by way of experiment, in addition to the art of angling, the cruelest, the coldest, and the stupidest of pretend sports. They may talk about the beauties of Nature, but the angler merely thinks of his dish of fish; he has no leisure to take his eyes from off the streams, and a single *bite* is worth to him more than all the scenery around. Besides, some fish bite best on a rainy day. The whale, the shark, and the tunny fishery have somewhat of noble and perilous in them; even net fishing, trawling, etc., are more humane and useful - but angling! No angler can be a good man.

LORD BYRON
Note to *Don Juan*

60

In Dr Crull's *Present State of Muscovy* (1698), mention is made of a pike that, when taken, was found to have an infant child in its stomach.

JONATHAN COUCH
A History of British Fishes, 1862

To boil a PIKE with pudding in the belly

Take out the gills and guts, wash it well, then make a good forcemeat of oysters chopped fine, the crumbs of half a penny loaf, a few sweet herbs, and a little lemon peel shred fine, nutmeg, pepper, and salt to your taste, a good lump of butter, the yokes of two eggs, mix them well together, and put them in the belly of your fish, sew it up, skewer it round, put hard water in your fish-pan, add to it a tea cupful of vinegar, and a little salt: when it boils put in the fish; if it be a middle size, it will take half an hour's boiling: garnish it with walnuts and pickled barberries, serve it up with oyster sauce in a boat, and pour a little sauce on the pike. You may dress a roasted pike the same way.

ELIZABETH RAFFALD
The Experienced English Housekeeper, 1782

This dish of meat is too good for any but anglers, or very honest men.

IZAAK WALTON
The Compleat Angler

Go thou to the sea, and cast an hook, and take up the fish
that first cometh up.

ST. MATTHEW, XVII, 27

There's a special fascination about fishing a sunken wreck.
With its gaping weed-draped portholes, hatches and
funnels, a rusting hulk lying on the sea-bed provides ideal
shelter for many species of fish. Huge baleful-eyed conger
swim sinuously through the perpetual gloom inside the
shattered hull, or venture forth occasionally on their tide-
governed hunting forays. Among the toppled masts and
crumpled superstructure roam marauding groups of cod,
pollack, coalfish and sharp-fanged ling, weaving in and
out of the openings, and occasionally darting forward to
seize their prey. Behind sheltering draperies of weed,
shoals of plump red bream lurk and hover, cautiously
eyeing the murky tide-stirred water for larger predators.

It is an exciting and rugged form of sea angling, with a
well-deserved reputation for producing plenty of
specimen-sized fish - and even the occasional record
breaker.

HUGH STOKER
Sea Angling Hotspots

It's easy!

Bait is the real secret to success. Soft-shelled crabs are the bass's idea of *foie gras.* Other deadly baits include sprats, sand-eels and mackerel, cut into thin strips with the shiny side outwards. As long as the bait is fresh, catching fish is absurdly simple.

JONATHAN YOUNG
The Daily Telegraph, 7 August 1992

Without fear of contradiction, the assertion can be made that the Great Western Railway covers, or leads to, the finest sea-angling grounds which have yet been discovered in the four corners of the United Kingdom.

Whilst the Company have endeavoured to ensure correctness in the compilation of this Guide, it must be understood that they will not accept any liability for the information given . . .

Around the Coast with Rod and Line, 1925

In the night usually the best trouts bite and will rise ordinarily in the still deeps, but not so well in the streams.

JAMES CHETHAM
The Angler's Vade Mecum, 1681

Anderson v Alnwick District Council

A public right to take worms from the foreshore was recognised by the common law and could properly be described as ancillary to the right to fish.

LORD JUSTICE EVANS

Queen's Bench Divisional Court, 21 December 1992

Black Marlin

Then I saw a splash like a depth bomb, and the sword, and eye, and open lower-jaw and huge purple-black head of the black marlin. The whole top fin was out of the water looking as high as a full-rigged ship, and the whole scythe tail was out as he smashed at that tuna. The bill was as big around as a base-ball bat and slanted up, and as he grabbed the bait he sliced the ocean open wide. He was solid purple-black and he had an eye as big as a soup bowl. He was huge. I'd bet he'd go a thousand pounds.

ERNEST HEMINGWAY

To Have and Have Not

When to Fish

In hot, sunshiny weather, the evening and the morning. If the weather is cloudy, any part of the day will do.

In winter, the middle of the day.

When angling after a shower, get the wind to your back, if you can.

It is no use to angle when the earth is hot and dry, or the east or north winds blow strong and cold.

The Angler's Almanac and Pocket-Book, 1854

There's little to beat sea trout fishing at night if conditions are right. The fish are shy; very often they'll provide ample evidence of their presence but show no interest in your lure. On the Polly we fished with a nine-foot leader with a single dropper, using low-water double hooks, usually about size 10. The patterns that got best results were the old friends - Butcher, Dunkeld, Peter Ross, Zulu, Black Pennell. The sea trout didn't run very large, three or four pounds would be a very good fish; but even a one and a half pounder fizzing round the sea pool at full throttle was something that stayed in your memory.

> J. R. HARTLEY
> *Fly Fishing*

From June till November fish feed or bite best in the mornings and evenings; from November to May the middle of the day is best, unless the weather is remarkably warm or muggy, in that case you will meet with sport from daylight till dark: and again, during the summer, if the weather is dark and cloudy, or a warm drizzling rain falls, you may expect sport in the middle of the day, and till it is quite dark.

> T. F. SALTER
> *The Angler's Guide*, 1815

When cold winds blow, always angle in the deep holes that lie under the wind, or you will meet with little sport, for fish are susceptible of cold.

> T. F. SALTER
> *The Angler's Guide*, 1815

THINGS WORTH KNOWING

When not to fish

Trout do not take well with a falling barometer; before a storm; in a south wind on a hot day; with haze on the hills; in a hard dry wind and bright sun; on dark windy days without rain; in leaden-coloured water; when the fly is not on the water.

The Angler's Weather Signs

If sheep are feeding with their backs to the wind, expect rain.

Hoar frost - sign of rain.

Trees go dark before a storm.

Tulips and dandelions close up before rain.

When the leaves of trees curl and there is a wind from the south, it indicates rain.

Unusually clear atmosphere and distant objects clearly seen mean rain.

If gnats are plentiful in spring, expect a fine autumn.

If it rains before sunrise, expect a fine afternoon.

If the chaffinch often repeats its call-note 'Pink,' it foretells rain.

How to Feed Worms

Not one of the many books I have read on angling tells how to feed worms, although they mostly note that worms can be kept for a time in moss. Worms can be kept for months in a box containing old, withered leaves and a little manure. All worms feed well on the old leaves, and if you will add a few tea-leaves all the better.

PAT CASTLE
Trout and How to Catch Them

What angler has not felt a cutting wind on his back.
There is an old saying that 'the man who sits with his
back to a draught, faces the grave.'

E. MARSHALL-HARDY
Mirror of Angling, 1937

When the wind is in the east,
'Tis neither good for man nor beast;
When the wind is in the north,
The skilful fisher goes not forth;
When the wind is in the south,
It blows the bait in the fishes mouth;
When the wind is in the west,
Then 'tis at the very best.

ANON.

I shall stay him no longer to wish him a rainy evening to read this following discourse; and that if he be an honest angler, the east wind may never blow when he goes a-fishing.

    IZAAK WALTON
    The Compleat Angler

For as to the Heat in Summer and Frost and Snow in Winter, he had better make Hay in One, and sit by the Fire in the other.

    ROBERT NOBBES, 1682

Cold winds and wretched weather which send the trout-fisher home empty-handed, seem to make little or no difference to the salmon. No day and no weather is hopeless, if there are salmon in the pools, but a fresh and even strong wind is usually a good thing for the salmon-fisher. Even bitter north and east winds do not prevent the fish from taking the fly.

    A. H. CHAYTOR
    Letters to Salmon Fisher's Sons

December

Chub, Roach, Jack and Pike continue to afford the angler amusement and profit, if a favourable opportunity offers to exercise his skill, which seldom occurs this month, as the waters are generally too thick, or frozen up.

    T. F. SALTER
    The Angler's Guide, 1815

If the air is cold and raw, the wind high, the water rough, or if the weather is wet, it is totally useless to angle in the Thames.

THOMAS BEST
A Concise Treatise on the Art of Angling, 1787

Why does a man say he has been fishing when he hasn't caught a thing.

ANON.

Some people are under the impression that all that is required to make a good fisherman is the ability to tell lies easily and without blushing; but this is a mistake. Mere bald fabrication is useless; the veriest tyro can manage that. It is in the circumstantial detail, the embellishing touches of probability, the general air of scrupulous - almost of pedantic - veracity, that the experienced angler is seen.

Fisherman's Licence

JEROME K. JEROME
Three Men in a Boat

An honest fisherman is a pretty uninteresting person.
   ANON.

Better be a poor fisherman than have to do with the
governing of men.
   DANTON

Confidence - the single most important item an angler
needs. Without this essential requirement, many fish
otherwise taken, will be lost.
   PETER LIGHTFOOT & KEVIN WHAY
   Stillwater Trout Fly-Fishers' Ready Reference

Let the blessing of St Peter's Master be . . . upon all that
are lovers of virtue; and dare trust in His providence; and
be quiet; and go a-Angling.
   IZAAK WALTON
   The Compleat Angler

Remember that it is water knowledge that catches the
fish, and the more an angler learns of his rivers, or the sea,
the more he can expect to catch.
   TREVOR HOUSBY
   The Art of Angling

I have always attempted to elevate fishing to the plane of an exact science. The man who *thinks* 'fish and fishing' must ultimately succeed in catching more fish than the man who leaves it to luck.

> T. C. IVENS
> *Still Water Fly Fishing*

Ever let your hook be hanging; where you least believe it, there will be a fish in the stream.

> OVID
> *Ars Amatoria*

Beware of Barbel

Their Spawn is surfeiting and dangerous, and whoever eats thereof, will break out in Blotches, and red Spots, will loath his Meat, lose his Appetite, and be extremely disorder'd. His liver is likewise unwholesome.

> GEORGE SMITH
> *The Gentleman Angler*, 1726

It is quite possible that like every other coarse fisherman you will commence your fishing by catching a small perch, roach or gudgeon, and the memory of this event is something that is liable to remain with you for the rest of your life.

> TAG BARNES
> *Coarse Fishing for Absolute Beginners*

Minnows were not despised, gudgeon were greeted with rapture, and the occasional triumph of a roach, with gorgeous red eyes, was a thing beyond words.

> H. T. SHERINGHAM
> *An Open Creel*

In a gastronomic point of view, *gobio* gives precedence to none: a fry of fat gudgeon, eaten piping hot, with a squeeze of lemon-juice, is a dish 'to set before a King,' and as superior to anything that Greenwich or Blackwall can produce, as Mouet's champagne is to gooseberry pop.

> H. CHOLMONDELEY-PENNELL
> *Fishing Gossip, 1886*

The Chub is in temper much like a pig, for if you want him to go one way, pull him the contrary, and you will commonly accomplish your object.

> JOHN BADDELEY
> *The London Angler's Book*, 1834

72

One of the most deadly baits for chub is wasp grub. In fact it is so good that most Midland associations have banned its use in matches.

> KEN COPE
> *The Angling Times Book of the Severn*

A new fashion among young professionals to hunt carp, the prime coarse fish that can grow to more than 50lbs, is one reason why Britain's angling industry, which nets £100 million in annual sales is seeing continued growth this year, despite the recession.

> DEREK HARRIS
> *The Times*, 3 August 1992

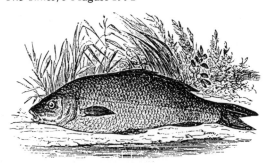

Carp Fishing

It's going to be a perfect summer evening. The breeze has dropped altogether, the pool is like a mirror, the sky is clear, the birds are enthusiastic about everything, the air smells of sun-baked grass and watermint - and *there*, even as I'm droning on, your line is beginning to tighten . . .

> CHRIS YATES
> *Specimen Hunter's Handbook*

The *Carp* is a fish that will teach an angler the value of patience, as he is endowed with extraordinary policy.

    The Art of Angling, 1812

The longevity of fish is greater than other creatures, and much surpasses the age of man; for it is well authenticated that in the royal ponds at Marli, in France, there are Carp which have been tamed, and preserved since the reign of Francis the First.

    T. F. SALTER
    The Angler's Guide, 1815

The Carp is the most crafty of fresh water fish, originally a foreigner, has a fleshy palate and leather mouth, a strong, broad, large scale, the fins blackish; when stewed with red wine, they are considered very good.

    JOHN BADDELEY
    The London Angler's Book, 1834

In one Day we caught about twenty brace of extraordinary large *Carps* with very sweet *Eeles* and *Tench*; I believe I shall hardly forget the *Pearch* of eighteen Inches long, caught by Capt. Comer, nor the Old Gentleman's resolution, while we were drinking a Dram of the Bottle, a Fish run away with his Rod, which he being unwilling to loose, stript off his Cloaths and leapt in, and in swimming proved too nimble for the fish, for I assure you, he brought them both out with much content to regain his Rod.

    JOHN WHITNEY
    The Genteel Recreation:
    Or, the Pleasure of Angling, 1700

When fishing on a river bank the last words in Walton's
Compleat Angler are to be strictly observed, viz., 'study to
be quiet,' for violent disturbance or motion is fatal to
sport.

    Encyclopaedia Britannica, 1875

Stephen Pritchard, the fishing-tackle maker of Builth,
caught, on Thursday last, in the course of four hours, no
less than 143 grayling, trout, and salmon-pink; and in five
hours on the following day, 225 fish of the same
description.

    Gloucester Journal, April 1838

Angler tread soft, for if the ground
By ruder feet make any sound;
Then void is all your care,
As well as if you stood too near:
Which to prevent no shadow should come nigh,
Nor you to see,
Where fishes be,
Into the waters pry;
Keep the Sun constant in your face,
Reflections on the water less will be,
So you'll have pleasure to embrace,
While others loose by their simplicity.

> JOHN WHITNEY
> *The Genteel Recreation:*
> *Or, the Pleasure of Angling,* 1700

Thursday, 18 July 1878
Hotter and hotter. My Father and I went to Talyllyn to
fish in Llangorse Lake. About noon we got into a shoal of
perch and killed 5 dozen or more in 2 hours, not large
ones. We pulled them out as fast as we could put the lines
in.

> *Kilvert's Diary*

The neighbourhood of Streatley and Goring is a great fishing centre. There is some excellent fishing to be had here. The river abounds in pike, roach, gudgeon, and eels, just here; and you can sit and fish for them all day. Some people do. They never catch them. I never knew anybody catch anything up the Thames, except minnows and dead cats, but that has nothing to do, of course, with fishing! The local fisherman's guide doesn't say a word about catching anything. All it says is the place is 'a good station for fishing', and from what I have seen of the district, I am quite prepared to bear out this statement.

There is no spot in the world where you can get more fishing, or where you can fish for a longer period. Some fishermen come here and fish for a day, and others stop and fish for a month. You can hang on and fish for a year, if you want to: it will be all the same.

The *Angler's Guide to the Thames* says that 'jack and perch are also to be had about here', but there the *Angler's Guide* is wrong. Jack and perch may *be* about there. Indeed, I know for a fact that they are. You can *see* them there in shoals, when you are out for a walk along the banks; they come and stand half out of the water with their mouths open for biscuits. And, if you go for a bathe, they crowd round, and get in your way and irritate you. But they are not to be 'had' by a bit of worm on the end of a hook, nor anything like it - not they!

JEROME K. JEROME
Three Men in a Boat

The perch is second only to the pike in boldness and voracity.

LORENZO PROUTY
Fish: Their Habits and Haunts and the
Methods of Catching Them, 1883

I think the Perch is the most beautiful of our fresh-water fish; he is dressed in a lovely combination of colours - red fins, deep green back, shading into a greenish-yellow on the sides, striped transversely with broad dark bands. He has a prickly fin on his back, and anglers have to be careful how they handle him, or they may get a sharp prick.

REVD. CHARLES A. HALL
The Open Book of Nature, 1919

Sturgeon occasionally come up the Thames, but they were never numerous in this river. Provision was made in ancient Acts excepting them from the vulgar fate of other fish, and in the instructions to the City water-bailiffs for the time being, orders were issued that the sturgeon 'was not to be secreted', and that all royal fishes taken within the jurisdiction of the Lord Mayor of London, as namely, whales, sturgeons, porpoises, and such like, should be made known, and the name and names of all such persons as shall take them shall be sent in to the Lord Mayor of London for the time being. The sturgeon therefore is always, when taken, sent direct to grace the table of majesty.

CHARLES DICKENS
A Dictionary of the Thames, 1880

A man may fish with the worm that hath eat of the King,
and eat of a fish that hath fed of the worm.

> SHAKESPEARE
> *Hamlet*

Clear water worm fishing is a branch of the art which
teaches as no other can the way of the trout.

> SYDNEY SPENCER
> *Clear Water Trout Fishing with Worm*

Angling: Impaling worms to catch fish.

> GEORGE COLMAN

Mr Jeremy stuck his pole into the mud and fastened his
boat to it.

Then he settled himself cross-legged and arranged his
fishing tackle. He had the dearest little red float. His rod
was a tough stalk of grass, his line was a fine long white
horse-hair, and he tied a little wriggling worm at the end.

> BEATRIX POTTER
> *The Tale of Mr Jeremy Fisher*

I am, Sir, a Brother of the Angle.

> IZAAK WALTON
> *The Compleat Angler*

She [Maggie] had told Tom, however, that she should like him to put the worms on the hook for her, although she accepted his word when he assured her that the worms couldn't feel (it was Tom's private opinion that it didn't much matter if they did). He knew all about worms and fish and those things.

GEORGE ELIOT
The Mill on the Floss

During the 1964 General Election campaign Mr Selwyn Lloyd told me that I should not describe myself as a 'fisherman' but as an 'angler'. There were, he said, 50,000 fishermen with a vote, as against 3,000,000 anglers, and that preponderance should not be ignored.

LORD HOME
Border Reflections

Caution is a most valuable asset in fishing, especially if you're the fish.

ANON.

Anglers are not otters, not seine nets, not fish-catching machines alone. This would be to deny the richness of the sport that has become in part an art form.

JOHN BAILEY
The Great Anglers

'No fish in there, old pig,' said the otter cheerfully, 'and don't say there are 'cos there ain't. Must have driven them away with all the swimming practice of yours.'

'What's a pig doing swimming anyway old duck?'

'I taught him,' said Felicity shortly. 'What's your name, if I might ask?'

'Izaak,' said the otter. 'And don't think it ain't 'cos it is.'

Felicity's eyes began to twinkle. 'Izaak?' she said. 'After Izaak Walton?'

'Who's he old duck?' said the otter.

'Oh, another famous fisherman,' said Felicity and she made her quot-quot-quotting noise.

'Never heard of him,' said the otter, 'and I know all the otters hereabouts and don't say I don't 'cos I do.'

> DICK KING-SMITH
> *Daggie Dogfoot*

Angling may be said to be so like the mathematics, that it can never be fully learnt.

> IZAAK WALTON
> *The Compleat Angler*

A Fisherman can rarely cross a bridge without lingering for a few moments to gaze upon the streams. Running water is a thing that fascinates and holds us spellbound.

> HAROLD RUSSELL
> *Chalkstream and Moorland*, 1911

When a man has resolved to give himself a fishing holiday, he should first fix a date for starting, and afterwards publish the fact abroad . . . It would be well also to insert a paragraph in the columns devoted to fashionable intelligence, which ought in itself to give the matter enough publicity to ensure the attention of the clerk of the weather, whose business it is to frustrate all that man proposes, and to turn on the east wind to that end. But the angler, having done all that is here counselled, should unostentatiously and without much luggage depart a week earlier than the date announced; so should he catch the wind in the south and plenty of fly on the river while the unsuspecting official is busy arranging a little cyclone or a trifling displacement of water in America, just to keep his hand in.

H.T. SHERINGHAM
An Open Creel

Fisherman - One who drops the fish a line but seldom hears from them.

ANON.

It has been said that man degenerates without frequent communion with nature. It certainly is true that this communion increases his reverence for and his appreciation of the beautiful in nature.

LORENZO PROUTY
Fish: Their Habits and Haunts and the Methods of Catching Them, 1883

Does not much of the delight of angling spring from the
peace and calm associated with placid lakes?

GARTH CHRISTIAN
Tomorrow's Countryside

Wednesday, 22 June 1870
The weather was too dry and hot for fishing, the fish were
sulky or sick, and all we caught were five little perch. To
me, however, the fishing was of little consequence. The
beauty of the evening and the Lake was extraordinary,
and in the west the Fan stood grand and blue and peaked
like a volcano.

Kilvert's Diary

 . . . Tom and Huck asked him to hold on a minute; they stepped to a promising nook in the riverbank and threw in their lines; almost immediately they had reward. Joe had not had time to get impatient before they were back again with some handsome bass, a couple of sun perch and a small catfish.

> MARK TWAIN
> *The Adventures of Tom Sawyer*

I love any discourse of rivers, and fish and fishing.

> IZAAK WALTON
> *The Compleat Angler*

To Know All About Fish

Whosoever desires to know all the abstruse Notions and Properties of Fish, let them diligently peruse and read the following Authors, viz: *Gesner, Rondelctius, Oribatius, lib 7, cap. 22 Monsieur Muffetus, Janus Dubatius, Aldrovandus, Franciscus Bonsvetus, Paulus Jovius, cap. 34, Pliny's Natural History, Bellonius, Hyppolitus Salvianus, Aristotle.*

> JAMES CHETHAM
> *The Angler's Vade Mecum*, 1681

Fish say, they have their stream and pond;
But is there anything beyond?

> RUPERT BROOKE

An Angler's View

Dearer than wild cataracts or Alpine glens are the still hidden streams which Bewick has immortalised in his vignettes, and Creswick in his pictures; the long glassy shallows, paved with yellow gravel, where he wades up between the low walls of fern-fringed rock, beneath nut, and oak, and alder, to the low bar over which the stream comes swirling and dimpling, as the water ouzel flits piping before him, and the murmur of the ringdove comes soft and sleepy through the wood. There, as he wades, he sees a hundred sights and hears a hundred tones, which are hidden from the traveller on the dusty highway above.

The traveller fancies that he has seen the country. So he has; the outside of it, at least; but the angler only sees the inside. The angler only is brought close face to face with the flower, and the bird, and the insect life of the rich river banks, the only part of the landscape where the hand of man has never interfered, and the only part in general which never feels the drought of summer, 'the trees planted by the waterside whose leaf shall not wither'.

CHARLES KINGSLEY
Chalkstream Studies

The Fish

Although you hide in the ebb and flow
Of the pale tide when the moon has set,
The people of the coming days will know
About the casting of my net,
And how you have leaped times out of mind
Over the little silver cords
And think that you were hard and unkind,
And blame you with many bitter words.

W.B. YEATS
Collected Poems

Your born angler is like a hound that scents no game but
which he is in pursuit of.

JOHN BURROUGHS

Angling is somewhat like poetry, men are to be born so.

IZAAK WALTON
The Compleat Angler

If it's ill work fishing when the fish'll no' take; and its
worse when they're no' there.

LORD GREY OF FALLODON

Game Warden: Are the fish biting today?
Weary Angler: I don't know. If they are, they're biting
                each other.

    ANON.

The float is pleasing in appearance,
and even more pleasing in disappearance.
        H.T. SHERINGHAM
        Angler's Hours

With the modern angler it may be taken as an axiom that
his sport is not what is popularly called *luck*, but varies
directly as his judgment; and as a corollary, it may be
added that, provided he is a keen and accurate observer,
his judgment will vary directly as his experience,
tempered by his capacity of execution.
        F.M. HALFORD
        Dry-Fly Fishing in Theory and Practice, 1889

Remember that the Wit and Invention of Mankind were bestowed for other Purposes than to deceive silly Fish; and that however delightful Angling may be, it ceases to be innocent when used otherwise than as a mere Recreation.

RICHARD BROOKES, 1766

There were three of us, our baggage as follows: Item, one bottle of gin, two shirts; Item, one bottle schnapps, two pairs stockings; Item, one bottle schiedan, one pair of fishing pants; Item, one bottle genuine aromatic, by Udolpho Wolfe, name on the wrapper, without which the article is fictitious, one pair of extra boots; Item, one bottle extract of juniper-berry; one bottle brandy, long and wide, prescribed by scientific skill for medical purposes. Also, rods, tackle in abundance, and a supply of gin; in addition, each of us had a quart-flask in our pockets, containing gin. We also had some gin inside when we started.

THOMAS NORRIS
American Angler's Book, 1864

Fishing lines are made of gut, twisted horse or cow's hair, and a single horse hair; also of silk and mohair, or of silk alone, either twisted or platted; those made of gut are the strongest, the twisted hair the cheapest, and the single horse-hair the finest.

T.F. SALTER
The Angler's Guide, 1815

Sound Advice

It is exceedingly desirable that the angler should be able to make and repair his own tackle. This will probably save him quite one-half of his outlay, and has the satisfaction of knowing that he can trust to the tackle, which he cannot always when he buys it; which, in case of accident, he can repair without delay, when the impossibility of doing so might peril his day's sport.

Encyclopaedia Britannica, 1875

Accustom yourself to use fine tackle, which will the sooner make you a skilful angler by greater care being requisite in using it: if you perchance to break your tackle, do not loose your temper, but sit down, and diligently repair the damage done, and begin again, recollecting that 'Hope and Patience support the Fisherman.'

T.F. SALTER
The Angler's Guide, 1815

If you pull out the Eyes of such Fishes as you catch, and fish with them, you will find them good Baits.

The Complete Family-piece, 1736

The eyes and spawn of fish were held legitimate lures as were cow's brains and pastes of strange composition, some of which were rendered more attractive of oil of ivory and other unguents.

A.S. TURBERVILLE
Johnson's England

I have always felt extremely disgusted at what is called preserved waters (except fish ponds); that is, where fish in these waters are claimed exclusively as private property. The disposition which sets up claims of this kind is the same as would - if it could - sell the sea and the use of the sun and the rain. Here the angler is debarred by the surly, selfish owner of the adjoining land, the pleasure of enjoying the most healthful and comparatively the most innocent of all diversions. It unbends the minds of the sedentary and the studious, whether it may be those employed at their desks, or 'the pale artist plying his sticky trade,' and enables such to return to their advocations, or their studies, with renovated energy, to labour for their own or for the public good.

THOMAS BEWICK (1753-1828)
Memoir, 1862

Trespass

If I go on another man's ground without licence, the owner may have an action of trespass against me; and if I continue there after warning by the owner or his servant thereunto authorised, the owner or his servant by his command, may put me off by force; but not beat me, unless I make resistance; 9th Edward IV. No servant shall be questioned for killing a trespasser within his master's liberty, who will not yield, if not done out of former malice: yet if the trespasser kills any servant, it is murder: 21st Elizabeth.

> T.F. SALTER
> *The Angler's Guide*, 1825

Vous auriez dû voir celui qui s'est échappé.

No man can lose what he never had.

> IZAAK WALTON
> *The Compleat Angler*

Nothing that is very new can be said about the method of angling. It is an old-fashioned art, and is still pursued after the mode that prevailed when Izaak Walton wandered, rod in hand, in the flowery meads that bordered the river Lea. Anglers, like poets, must be born to their vocation.

> ANTHONY TROLLOPE (ed.)
> *British Sports and Pastimes*

To prevent disputes, it is generally understood and agreed among anglers, that a distance the length of rod and line, or thirty feet, shall be kept between each person while angling.

T.F. SALTER
The Angler's Guide, 1815

The ultimate epitaph
An excellent angler, and now with God.
IZAAK WALTON
The Compleat Angler

Often after walking a mile or two on the way to the river, at a brisk pace, there comes upon one a feeling of fitness, of being made of nothing but health and strength so perfect, that life need have no other end but to enjoy them. The pure act of breathing at such times seems glorious. People talk of being a child of nature, and moments such as these times when it is possible to feel so; to know the full joy of animal life - to desire nothing beyond. There are times when I have stood still for the joy of it all, on my way through the wild freedom of a Highland moor, and felt the wind, and looked upon the mountains and water and light, till I felt conscious only of the strength of a mighty current of life, which swept away all consciousness of self, and made me a part of all that I beheld.

LORD GREY OF FALLODON
Fly-fishing, 1899

Finally, to all honest anglers a word of advice - Fish fair, never take undersized or ill-conditioned fish, never refuse to brother angler a day's fishing or a pattern fly, and give freely and fully as I have endeavoured to do the benefit of any discovery you have made or experience you have gained in the great case of 'Angler v Fish.'

F.M. HALFORD
Dry-Fly Fishing in Theory and Practice

To fish is to meld with nature. You are no longer just an observer of its beauty, a visitor in a strange land; you become part of the wild.

JOHN FITZPATRICK
Evening Standard, 24 February 1993

It must be apparent to every experienced fisherman, that angling is a science in which some portion of fresh knowledge may ever be acquired.

PISCATOR
The Practical Angler, 1842

Next time!

Next time we shall be more skilled, more fortunate. Next time! To-morrow, and to-morrow, and to-morrow. Grey hairs come, and stiff limbs, and shortened sight; but the spring is green and hope is fresh for all changes in the world and in ourselves.

ANDREW LANG
Angling Sketches, 1891